Praise for *Sentenced to Venice*

"The masterful collection you hold in your hands is a ticket to Venice past and present. You will be transported by 'wings wide open but unmoving,' will travel in the company of poems so beautifully rendered you won't notice each is only one sentence long…such is the remarkable skill of the poet. Each poem lives as though boundless, boundary-less, complete, rich in description, history, celebration and longing as, with Huck, we both 'break through the bright vault of heaven' and mourn with the poet the passing of time: 'Like you Venice I once ruled the corner of the earth…and now I seek no greater later years than yours.'"
-Ellen Waterston, author of *Hotel Domilocos*

"*Sentenced to Venice* provides both a cultural critique of life in the serene Republic, and a poignant reflection on mortality. Huck gives us artists and patrons, Casanova and Mozart, John the Baptist and a parade of saints, courtesans and ladies of the night, even the dogs and cats that accompany her tour of ancient sites and the ever-present canals. She engages meticulous historical research, while constantly balancing the past with the nearness of the present condition. Her poetic insights reach deep into the psyche with language that has the "molten clarity" of glass. Her wit and wry sense of humor soften the tragic tales that engulf the city, while she artfully arranges each poem in a single vibrant sentence. These poems 'flicker like memory/ above gondolas sliding through luscious dark.' The final poem in the collection pleads, "grant my penance be walking these four/hundred and nine bridges… as I climb over water each day// toward heaven." It is a journey that has unveiled 'masks and secrets,' that has earned a profound reverie."
-Carol Barrett, Ph.D., author of *Calling in the Bones* and *Pansies*

"In *Sentenced to Venice*, Kake Huck—deep-seeing and witty poet-guide as female Virgil—lights our way into the glittering past and present of this 'Most Serene City' that seethes beneath with hungers and flaws. Her artfully compressed poems illuminate the journey in soundwork and sensual imagery—the succulence of a stolen lemon, a 'scarlet anemone blown like/a bursting heart' in glass, the 'bright vault of broken heavens.' From Casanova to St. Augustine, Titian to Pollock, she lays open for us the perpetual play (or war) among art, sex, religion, and politics, her sharp observations drawing into focus the disparity between artifice and reality. And yet the poems are also threaded through with the personal: running like the aqua alta that slowly dooms the city with inundation is her awareness of the inexorable passage of time, the close cut of mortality in herself and one she loves. A passionate collection of appreciation, exposure, and confession, this book invites us to keep Huck company as she 'climb[s] over water each day//toward heaven' in these compelling poems."
-Judy Montgomery, author of *Pulse & Constellation*

"Kake Huck's, *Sentenced to Venice*, is a quirky, informed and irreverent homage to a great world city. Her poems, bursting with color, entertain and instruct (as hinted by the book's title) in a dexterous one sentence format. The book's deft treatment of Venice's characters, history, art and architecture can serve as a proper baedeker for visitors, yet does not avoid life's eternal questions that lurk in the doorways of Venice, thus fulfilling poetry's eternal promise."
-Marion Davidson, author of *Closeness of Ice*

Sentenced to Venice

poems

KAKE HUCK

Sentenced to Venice
copyright © Kake Huck 2019
First Edition

All rights reserved. No part of this publication may be reproduced, stored in, or introduced into a retrieval system, or transmitted in any form, or by any means (electronic, mechanical, photocopying, recording, or otherwise) without the prior written permission of the author, except in the case of brief quotations or sample images embedded in critical articles or reviews.

Paperback ISBN: 978-1-945587-37-5
Library of Congress Control Number: 2019910955
Kake Huck
Sentenced to Venice

Book design: Dancing Moon Press
Cover design: Lindy Martin
Manufactured in the United States of America
Dancing Moon Press
www.dancingmoonpress.com

The poem, "Pinecones, Venice" was previously published in a collection called *Last Call: The Anthology of Beer, Wine & Spirits Poetry*, edited by James Bertolino.

The poem, "One Afternoon at Santa Lucia Train Station" was previously published in *Women on the Brink: Stories*, by G. Elizabeth Kretchmer.

To Will

...and many thanks to the Skyhooks
for their years of thorough critique.

TABLE OF CONTENTS

SENTENCED TO VENICE	x

PART I: TIME PAST — 1

A FEW NOTES ON THE BEGINNING OF THE TOURIST INDUSTRY IN 17TH CENTURY VENICE	2
CHOPINES	3
SAINT MARK, LION OF VENICE	4
GIOVANNI BATTISTA BENEDETTI (b. Venice 1530 d. Turin 1590)	5
IN 1819 THE ELEPHANT	6
HISTORICAL RIDDLE	7
CASANOVA AT HIS DESK, 1775	8
CASANOVA IN CHILDHOOD	9
CASANOVA AT 50	10
CASANOVA MEETS MOZART AT THE PREMIER OF *DON GIOVANNI* IN PRAGUE, 1787	11
CASTING IRON BEFORE THE GHETTO	12
WAITING FOR VIRGIL	13
WHITE SWAN OF CITIES	14

PART II: EKPHRASTICALLY SPEAKING — 15

ST. AUGUSTINE IN HIS STUDY BY Vittore Carpaccio	16
JACOB'S LADDER BY TINTORRETO	17
PATRONAGE	18
THE PENTECOST MOSAIC AT ST MARK'S BASILLICA	19
BOOKWORM IN *PARADISO*	*20*
PRESENTATION OF *THE VIRGIN IN THE TEMPLE* (1538)	21
THE BETRAYER'S ERASURE	22
KNOCKED ON MY GLASS	23
TOURING THE PALAZZOS	24
THE LOGO OF VENICE	25

PART III: IS TIME PRESENT — 27

THE HAZARD OF LOVING	28
VEDUTA	30
OF DEATH IN VENICE	31
SHOWROOM NEAR THE MURANO FACTORIES	32

AT MUSEO DI STORIA NATURAL DI VENEZIA ON THE GRAND CANAL	33
WALKING MEDITATION	34
CONVERSATION ON A VAPORETTO	35
PASSAGGIATA STORIES	36
ONE AFTERNOON AT SANTA LUCIA TRAIN STATION	37
One of those Anagram Poems of the Sort Taught in Writer's Workshops and used when the writer has run short of ideas	38
MY FAVORITE ROOM AT PEGGY GUGENHEIM'S	39
DYING ROOMS OF LIGHT	41
MORNING PRACTICE	42
COMMISSARIO GUIDO BRUNETTI	43
THIS, OF COURSE, IS HOW	45
IN PRAISE OF THE SURFACE	46
TOURIST RUMINATION	47
MORTALITY	48
THE DEATH OF VENICE	49

PART IV: AT LEAST BACK HOME   51

OF COURSE THE IMPOSSIBLE BEAUTY	52
GOOGLE EARTH AND THE SERENE REPUBLIC	53
PINECONES, VENICE	54
LIKE YOU, VENICE	55
BUT NOT YET, OH VENICE	56
SENTENCED TO VENICE, YET,	57
About the Author	59

Kake Huck

SENTENCED TO VENICE

for crimes against the giant western sky --
blue blanket cast across the open space
that fills our lives, great arc of frozen grace
holding us with the promise we can fly

someday away from all that binds, untie
the locks of love and family, learn to embrace
our changing lives, the always upward race
to more freedom, more happiness, that high

that is America but isn't where
I find a heart so hungry for the past
it seeks small squares of stone, rejects the vast
azure avowal, looks up instead to air

made close with history and sea, bright vault
of broken heaven, absolving all my faults.

PART I: TIME PAST

Kake Huck

A FEW NOTES ON THE BEGINNING OF THE TOURIST INDUSTRY IN 17TH CENTURY VENICE

At end of shipbuilding, the end of war,
(pluck the lute, tap tap the *spinetta*)
Venetians sought new source of gold
(sing Monteverdi's madrigals)

so sold their city with oars and whores
(blow bright on flute, swoon sweet the *cornetto*)
lengthening *Carnevale* so more could be sold
of meat and sweets and boys and girls

to travelers from more Protestant lands
who found the Papist customs odd;
admired and despised a forgiving God
Who saw past the sins of celebration

all things allowed beneath the masks
that disappeared under Wednesday's Ash.

CHOPINES

The year da Vinci painted *Mona Lisa*
a teenage prostitute wobbled along
Venetian sidewalks, small feet

cupped in these souring shoes,
crystal-crusted velvet nailed
to leather platforms, a man's

handspan of cork beneath
each foot, a fashion shared with
noble ladies with no need to walk

to work, no need to let hip sway and
stumble advertise the wares of one
of twelve thousand selling

pleasure near these old canals,
keeping bodies balanced above
dung and sea-water glazed stone

salizada, perhaps stopping in one
of the city's hundred churches
on their promenade.

Kake Huck

SAINT MARK, LION OF VENICE

Seven centuries after the mob
    dragged you heavenward on Alexandrian streets,

Venetian merchants stole your uncorrupted corpse,
sheathed it in swine flesh to distract
the sentries of the Caliphate,

    and sailed home to entomb
your holy remnants (now washed one hopes)
beside the doge's palace, giving their young Republic

    celestial cachet

for war and commerce while
transfiguring your evangelism into a sales pitch

for the feudal tourist trade.

Sentenced to Venice

GIOVANNI BATTISTA BENEDETTI (B. VENICE 1530 D. TURIN 1590)

for Sean

Tartaglia your tutor told *tuo padre*
that your path
(not unlike his own) was math,
its almost secret magics
of accountancy and war
sure route to wealth

but you, already rich
decided just to prove your
own bright calculus
for falling bodies
and their speed,

no need attending university
for classes you can teach;
instead you write
and lecture on hydraulics
and astronomy,
astrology and optics,

plus letters on the oscillation
of harmonic waves -- while stories
of your genius reach patrons with a
passion for some perfect predictability

underlying the brilliant chaos of their world.

Kake Huck

IN 1819 THE ELEPHANT

in Venice, captured for
distraction of the tourists
come for *Carneval*, great slave
confined while others of
his kidnapped herd
are elsewhere,
     resists his fate,
     trumpeting with rage,
     great heart a-crack:

thick legs remembering
thunder
   thunder
      thunder

crush his keeper,
carry him outside
to momentary freedom
where before his death
by canon fire
he broke into a fruit stall,
ate his fill
and met his fate
after a strong *caffe*.

HISTORICAL RIDDLE

When you look for yourself you see me
when I was watery then bold as bronze
as I screened Perseus from certain stone,

gave Paul his metaphor for earthly insight,
was present anywhere if polished but
quickly dulled until Venetian reinvention

as tin-mercury on glass made my massive
manufacture possible so everyone --
from slave with some small shattered sliver

to a master of some minor universe placing me
face to face across broad golden corridors
to fake infinity as though my endless optical echo

could cheat death and
see the meaning of *alone*.

Kake Huck

CASANOVA AT HIS DESK, 1775

Staring out at torches that flicker like memory
above gondolas sliding through luscious dark,
he adjusts his spine against green-velvet-covered
horsehair and slides dry fingers over the heavy
gilded c-scrolls that support his arms, thinking
about a girl he touched three decades past, now
present in a fragrant letter, cast in bad Italian,
lying underneath the curving golden *amorini*
that grip the candelabra on this desk the worthy
unmarried Dandolo gave him with the paltry
stipend that never quite covers what he's lost
at faro or his other favorite games.

CASANOVA IN CHILDHOOD

a thousand empty rooms before
intrigue, expected and surprised,
slipped in, broke in, barged in, money
in hand, wine in hand, ribbons
from barely fastened shell pink shift
just dropping off a creamy shoulder
                                in hand,
cocked and loaded pistol
                                in hand,
jeweled stiletto, rusty dagger or pike
                                in hand

                                while he,
the always ready, always waiting, never patient
sat silent, poised, purring like a
kitten in the Venice opera house
where Mother played and sang and ushered
gold-thick strangers into the room they
shared to teach a tiny boy how
empty rooms were never quite
as barren
                as they seemed.

Kake Huck

CASANOVA AT 50

He digs strong thumbs into thin rind,
breathes deep a burst of citrus scent
that covers the dead summer stench of
brackish water and wonders why
he cannot imagine those lovers of
his youth as aged and empty like
a lemon peel grown blue and white
with rot, and only sees them as he
wishes he were still: young, plump,
and fresh as this exquisite fruit just
plucked from that now fragrant tree
behind his neighbor's wall and
well-locked gate.

Sentenced to Venice

CASANOVA MEETS MOZART AT THE PREMIER OF *DON GIOVANNI* IN PRAGUE, 1787

Just half my age, this genius boy said
what he's heard of me sounds like his so-
called hero pulled to hell at opera's
end but I replied,

        "You might as well
name Venice, 'Spain,' and say that
friendship, gifts, persuasion,
and shared sensual joy –

great gifts of love's serene republic –

are just the same as tyranny and
oppressive courtly vice,
                a vile
comparison to someone who has
danced the masking of status
at *Carnevale* and still stays friends
with both maid and mistress
of palazzos off the Grand Canal.

Kake Huck

CASTING IRON BEFORE THE GHETTO

Flame-colored metal flowed here
before the foundries moved
and made way for the Jews

who like the ironworks they replaced
were needed but thought too dangerous
for close association and just as

molten steel is shaped within its cast,
becoming hinge, oar lock or blade,
so were the Chosen forced behind

the gates of this small urban island,
this *borghetto* – town within a town --
where they were useful financiers

who helped war-broken migrants
and royal gamblers before night
locked the gates around the

squares that gave the world
a new word for repression.

WAITING FOR VIRGIL

No dark woods ring the Serene City
surrounded by water, islands unlike
Florence, Dante's home, town without pity

that banished him not for words of delight
written for Beatrice long after she
was dead, but for vicious strikes

his party made against its foes, for
politics is always at the heart
of all, love unexcepted, and the key

to our long fight or truce (I can't now sort
out which it is) lies in these hidden woods
walled in our chests, spring petals within forts

(now finally free of military goods)
adrift on winter's final kiss; a pretty
storm of blossoms, torn off from their roots.

Kake Huck

WHITE SWAN OF CITIES

Longfellow called you,
imagining your heavy stone

      turned threaded white,

barely glimpsed among
          the reeds,
              a thing of flight

now nested, caught by nature's
      need to warm the future

until wet wings and knifing beak
                    crack

through the brittle membrane separating

      now

in all its waiting hush from

    next
      or
        in a moment

      or even
          suddenly

when

what was always promised
but lay hidden in desire
almost fulfilled
      bursts from its fragile home

to seek the
pillowed comfort

of your

absurd allure.

PART II: EKPHRASTICALLY SPEAKING

Kake Huck

ST. AUGUSTINE IN HIS STUDY BY VITTORE CARPACCIO

Books open on his desk and floor,
glass pen in hand, small Maltese dog
(fond sign of faithfulness seen
in Venetian oils) now waiting
patiently for finish of familiar
scratching nib on vellum and the
dusty walk that follows,

                        the Saint sits

among impossible possessions –
the Catholic mitre, crosier, and thurible
(absurd in ancient Africa) and
scientific instruments – an armillary
sphere and astrolabe, revealing

                        someone's

interest in a world made knowable to science
now caught in this unnatural light,
glazed windows aglow with Presence that
forestalls the writer's labor as he hears
                        across a thousand miles of desert

the dying whispers of Jerome, mentor and rival,

while several centuries after their creation
I recognize this moment of divided concentration
between man and dog and God.

JACOB'S LADDER BY TINTORRETO

On the ceiling of the Scuola Grande di San Rocco
Old Jacob dreams bright angels drifting
wings wide open but unmoving,
           afloat above his nodding head

on creamy stairs that lead in sharp
perspective upward toward rough gray clouds,
obscure disguise of a
           contraction of the infinity

of lift required by every dream that draws
us up
and up
into the bright explosive calm of light
and gold and almost unseen figure on His Throne

           before we tumble
back to russet, gray and umber wakefulness,
aware we've been invited, but never quite
sure where.

PATRONAGE

They put themselves in the picture over the altar,
la Abbadessa Elena Foscari et *la Priora* Marina Donato
two 15th Century noblewomen, politically connected
but unmarried, dwelling inside the convent walls
of San Zaccaria; watching over unwanted virgins
and patronizing local artists all too happy
to cast the one as *Sant'Elena*, mother of an
emperor and the other as Santa Marina,
(who lived most of her life as a man in
a monastery) two holy women providing
lessons in power, secrecy, and the importance
of being thought to wield *il peni*.

THE PENTECOST MOSAIC AT ST MARK'S BASILLICA

Here are the distant dead
made real through shining artifice

as gold tiles surrounding saintly
portraits now catch candle glow

as well as amplified Italian
recitation of Nicea's compromise

and share it with these en-domed
saints, the twelve who followed

hearts' compulsion, mosaic portraits
a polished circle above this rubber -

necking tourist caught within tradition,
looking from her knees to see those happy

men above, their heads alight with
fire and silver rays that bind them

to the pigeon in their center
on its throne.

Kake Huck

BOOKWORM IN *PARADISO*

(after the painting by Tintoretto)

In a public room of *Il Palazzo Ducale*,
 there among the multitude of *puti* wings
and pope's heads, of saints and prophets

whose portraits vibrate every inch of that
vast canvas covering an entire wall,
sits a saintly reader, half nude, his back to

Moses, his halo bent, eyes toward
the printed pages on his knees, bound
to the bound word, like us ignoring

the flood of flesh and angels rising,
                                              rising
to hear the golden conversation of
a mother and her son.

PRESENTATION OF *THE VIRGIN IN THE TEMPLE* (1538)

Under painted stone slab steps
nailed over our heads
                      inside the Academia,

an old woman cloaked
in blue and white, sits
fat and fierce
with heavy empty hands,
bushel basket on her left,
gazing right into the crowd

where Venice mimics Nazareth,
waiting for someone to fill
one upturned open fist with coins for eggs,

as unaware as we
                    of our own meaning,

that she is just a sign of sovereign
justice cast in colors of the Virgin girl
                    aglow over our heads:

Titian's illustrated oath
that this city harbored
                all

within its borders,
            even us.

Kake Huck

THE BETRAYER'S ERASURE

Just as *Doge* Marino Falier's portrait
in the *Sala del Maggior Consiglio*
was painted over after his head

bounced
        down
                the steps
of the Doge's Palace

(hacked off for betraying
a Republic that loved him)

so I've expunged your face
        from my great chamber of counsel,

removed your head
        from my newly serene city,

                      and
                      like those who expunged
                      the image of the 14th Century
        duke,

writ across the inner wall
where I once knew your face
a gilded admonition:

"Hic es locus decapitati pro criminibus".

KNOCKED ON MY GLASS

after Josiah McElheny's "Collection of Glass Concerning the Search for Infinity"

The time beyond my death,
the time before my birth,

swirls in white dots and rings
on clear dinner plates,

blown through a Bostonian's
Twenty First Century lips

into clear glass wheels
first shaped in Seventeenth

Century Venice on the heated
island of Murano where

hands and faces prevented
by threat of death from

carrying off the burning
secret of luminosity and shape
blushed, sweat and blistered

creating molten clarity,
turning and
       turning and
              turning through their fires

a measured presentation
of mathematical calculation

of humanity's ability
to seize on God's perfection.

Kake Huck

TOURING THE PALAZZOS

Every door opens to a room on either side
(each archway marks an exit and an entrance)

so though our guide may raise a brow or frown
I sometimes backtrack through the later groups –

the Deutsch and Brits in baggy sweaters,
the Japanese with all the latest gear –

until I find the work (that painting with a small white dog,
a bronzed myth burnished and alive with curls,
carved marble floor cut in concentric circles,

Renaissance architect's allusion to eternity)
the work I've promised myself I'll remember

even after we have walked beneath the final arch,
even after I have finally gone back home.

THE LOGO OF VENICE

standing *passant guardant*,
raised paw upon a book
with that angelic greeting,
"Pax tibi, Marce, Evangelista meus,"

carved into marble,
sewn onto flags,
melted into glass,
representing the Evangelist after

he has finished writing, died,
had his bones dug up, stolen,
and reburied
              before his image
grew to more than what he was:

a poor man writing beautiful stories
of Someone Else's past.

PART III: IS TIME PRESENT

Kake Huck

THE HAZARD OF LOVING

"A hazard of loving Venice is that poetic observations keep popping into one's head. . . . Uttering them should be resisted at any cost." Judith Martin

If we did not write about
what has already been written about
by those greater (or deader)
than ourselves

then we would write about
nothing because no
               thing is free
of observation that leads to de-
               scription which races
               toward metaphor

except those things
which indubitably are

but of those things
which are not, of course Venice is second only

to the moon or perhaps
the sea or perhaps
full lips curved into an eternal half-smile on a stone
bodhisattva
or painted in oil on a portrait of someone's mistress

but now, just now,
               settled on the face

of a slender woman in a green and gold dress
standing on the *Ponte del Diavolo*,
                        a bridge once crossed

by plague doctors in beaked masks

Sentenced to Venice

rushing to release the overabundant blood
of the dying, catching it like
        dark,
                red
                        ink.

Kake Huck

VEDUTA

for a suicide

I'll hide from you, Ghost, within my own *veduta* --
detailed cityscape, painter's quest for machine
perfection, photo-realism before the camera's
invention,
                    long views by Canaletto, Canal,
Bellotto, or Guardi, their people just thin
strokes of perfect, painted costumes,
giving scale to San Marco, the Grand Canal, the Palace –

so I become a few daubs of black,
a prick of white, a spit of crimson,
a small shadowed movement in the piazza,
unrecognizable without the thickened glass
your spectral hand will never raise up to
your drownéd eyes.

OF DEATH IN VENICE

Death news dwells on intermittent wifi
in *Albergo Marin* where my husband naps
after hours of old masters
                              while still charged up
I sit one floor below, tablet catching small waves
atumble over time and space and finger my past
in boredom until I track nostalgic Facebook
gossip to an unexpected death --

my high school drama coach (bright mentor,
fierce director, first gay man admired)
had somehow, though I pictured him as plump
and ruddy as he'd been,
                              turned old and sick
and gone a good five years before though
I'd still thought him living somewhere back
in orchards turned to server farms,

                          where someday
with my faded love in hand I'd see him again and
say I felt his presence in the masks and secrets
of the tourist city where I now

                            weep.

Kake Huck

SHOWROOM NEAR THE MURANO FACTORIES

Love flips on my crazy switch,
takes the wallet from my pocket,
the Visa from my wallet, and
judgment from a pre-frontal
cortex overwhelmed by possession-
triggered dopamine as I am seduced
to buy expensive beauty, to take home
a Wonderful Thing reminding me
of this fateful love so even though I
can't afford the finest statuary
I choose a costly yet clichéd *oggetto d'arte* --
reminder of that moment of surrender
when I dropped a grand (in Euros) on a
six-pound crystal lump of wave-form glass
with four shining fish forever frozen
over a scarlet anemone blown like
a bursting heart, tentacles waving
in suspended seas forever.

AT MUSEO DI STORIA NATURAL DI VENEZIA ON THE GRAND CANAL

"Vieni, ragazzi," chides the teacher
tour guide, hoping to move two blue-
jeaned teens away from the

great glistening plasma ball where
they still lean absentmindedly,
their gazes tangled, as spark strings
blister madly beneath warm hands

in witless warning that electricity
from elsewhere often awaits
an unthinking touch.

Kake Huck

WALKING MEDITATION

The infinite echo of other people's lives
is louder in stone streets between marble
palaces settled on sand made sturdy by a
thousand logs pounded down through marsh
over a thousand years ago, holding strong
through power and penitence, like
the love of God in the age of universal
tourism.

CONVERSATION ON A VAPORETTO

I don't know why I picked him," she says
to the man holding a small white dog

kicking its back legs against his
thick gray coat, small nails making thin

bright sounds against the shift-beat
background of water slapping against

the bright black bottom of our
wheel-less bus, now carrying this

couple, myself and three workmen,
out toward Murano, as she continues,

"Oh yes, I made the choice because
I missed the passion and thought he

might . . ." and then the voice slips under
engine grind as we rush through rain to

a town enwrapped in glass making fire.

Kake Huck

PASSAGGIATA STORIES

It's not a dance but a stroll
on the wide Zaterre,

broad *fondamenta* beside
the Giudecca Canal,

where custom brings
Venetians and their visitors

to saunter through evening air:
though tonight quick heel clicks

heard through dusk-soft voices,
heard above cruise ships rumble
heard like the distant barking

of an unhappy Italian dog,
signal some woman intent

on time and place and just
what else we must imagine,

filling her stranger's story
with love or death or

seafood cacciatori.

ONE AFTERNOON AT SANTA LUCIA TRAIN STATION

Two calico sisters, all bone
with age, are sleeping near the narrow
causeway that connects Venice, The Most
Serene, to Europe (so that the latter isn't lonely)
when one cat (the larger - a bit
of orange beneath her oval chin)
is startled by the noon-time
train's hot rush and reaches
for her ancient box-mate,
who is now already stretching
into elsewhere, leaning away
from the always forever
hunger of the other's need.

Kake Huck

One of those Anagram Poems of the Sort Taught in Writer's Workshops and used when the writer has run short of ideas

Venice by Twilight is a
thieving blew city, and blights
even icy wit so why elicit being tv
when twitchy begin evil,
twitchy being vile;
 so begin levity,
Witch, for by wit we
lighten vice and by wit
evince light.

Sentenced to Venice

MY FAVORITE ROOM AT PEGGY GUGENHEIM'S

Four Pollocks pulse above the marbled swamp,
spatter of modernity's enmeshed abandon
blazing in this space a bare five dogs across
in each direction, with each direction firing
above, below, beyond the boundaries set 600
years ago by merchants, bankers, financiers;
the wet and Most Serenne Republic's faithful
followers of (investors in) the markéd formal
line that captured gods and martyrs, porticos
and kings, Mary with her book, Europa with
her bull, Arabs, Africans, Jews, plates of fish,
oysters, pearls, lace, oranges beside a naked girl
or two and always that small dog in the corner,
guarding, eating, revealing that this art

SHOWS ME WHAT YOU'VE GOT,

made when what you got was some THING
when THINGS were what we all believed
in – those days when you knew that the
soldi with the face of the latest *doge* could
actually buy something instead of later,
later when Peggy, poorest of the Guggenheims,
bought these paintings on the cheap, bought
smeared effigies of FEELINGS, those
Black (red gray yellow green)
Red (gray black blue white)
Yellow (green black red)
Blue -- in the night kind of feelings that has
none of the weight of the marble beneath
your feet sinking two and a half centimeters
into the mud every year in tidal sure
deterioration, sea rising higher and
higher, *aqua* always more *alta* and we all know
as we gaze inches from these vibrating colors

Kake Huck

that this city can't be saved, that nothing
can be saved even these, these explosions
of the NOW that was then but is still,
still now.

DYING ROOMS OF LIGHT

Dark moss now crawls across a wall
within the first floor room of a
still rentable palazzo, where once
bright nymphs and gods,
whose youth and passion caught in paint
(now stripped and peeling into mold)
once glorified the lives of those
who loved beneath their dance
those days before the ever-rising sea

of time that takes us all,
                              us all,
rolled in,
            rolled in

with salt and waste and stink
                          and

and little fish aswim above
a stone mosaic floor with
lapis stars and crystal moons
now tombed beneath the
flood forever rising,
                rising

                          rising till it drowns us all.

Kake Huck

MORNING PRACTICE

Viola da gamba plum song slips
slow over alleys under morning
mist before stores slide clatter
doors and children shout awake
the day though so few so young
here among cannels where
all are busy being born to the
business of a city dying still
within the stillness of this
unseen benediction.

Sentenced to Venice

COMMISSARIO GUIDO BRUNETTI

for Donna Leon

like any central character of
some successful series soaked
in crime, can carry on his well-

dressed back more plot than
possible, more murders than
likely in his small city, Venice

of the post-ice age, Venice
of the tourist flood, Venice
long past,
        long past,
                long past

ascendency, those golden days
when war and secret censure
managed enemies within
and enemies without the

water wall that marked
Republic's edge until technology
made boundaries meaningless

saving that final line the law
would like us all to cross
by will of God instead of

someone else's urge, that
end which always in our
minds must justify the hours spent

with evidence, minutiae culled,
survivors grilled, all motives
ascertained until at last

Kake Huck

our savior, *Il Commissario*,
discovers the killer the none
of us foresaw, that all already

knew from our own birth.

THIS, OF COURSE, IS HOW

the dark at first appears
dangerous and imprecise
in the corners of a painting –

puddling perhaps around the feet
of some saint soon sacrificed
or over the shoulders of mythic

lovers half clothed in gold and
shining with desire – growing
only later into sharp-edged

shadows, measurable as midnight,
harmless at last while sliding down
mosaic hallways of the *pensione*

we call our life.

Kake Huck

IN PRAISE OF THE SURFACE

Those who know me only here
like this, wine glass or whiskey in
one hand, *cicchetti* in the other,
may think another self somewhere
abides, heavy hulled and riding deep
in ancient waters, soul of a poet or
philosopher, but I know better that
such depth can run aground, get
stuck, get cracked beyond repair
among these islands, these lives
thrown down together not by
design but through the accidents
of workplace weather, while
craft that glide across experience --
flat bottomed gondolas, curve prow,
enamel shiny, a single oar both power
and direction -- can skim and turn
and slide above life's muck unhampered
by uncertain measure of the water
waiting black beneath our feet.

Sentenced to Venice

TOURIST RUMINATION

Shopping alone near the Rialto
I realize I've almost forgotten how
to live without you

        (how to shop
        for a week of meals that are
        something more than ramen
        or do laundry, or return home at night
        to a lack of your ensorceling warmth)

and remembered my seven years
of midnight grocery runs,
vacuuming at 5 am,
dinners with *Cagney and Lacey*,

and always work
       and work
              and work

with dear colleagues who

    could not,

        who cannot,

tame the black dog who gallops
beside me, my hand in his teeth,
his nose deep in winter.

Kake Huck

MORTALITY

I wake in Venice wondering
if you are still alive and
listen for your breath, lift
on my elbow and stare
hard in meager moonlight
[or is it just the yellow gleam
above a nearby court where
Sudanese and German
youth still toss the ball
through ragged chains
attached to silvered hoops]
stare at the golden counterpane
above your ribs and only
close my eyes again after
I see your knuckles clutch
in sleep and pull its scarlet
patterns up across the aging
cage that holds our beating
heart.

THE DEATH OF VENICE

When you are at last
beneath the risen sea
with only second stories
of palazzos seen above
the wine dark waves

then may I ghostly drift
like dream through empty
marble halls, peer up past
shifting mirrored surface
of the air, my eyeless gaze

a gull in flight above
your broken, shining domes;
my earless heart a heron
standing in the ancient
silenced thunder of four

horses on St. Marks.

PART IV: AT LEAST BACK HOME

Kake Huck

OF COURSE THE IMPOSSIBLE BEAUTY

is always there in the now --
first horn chords call through
bitty ear-buds to some hunt

in the elsewhere; violin birds
trill through baroquen branches
before sweet minor oboe song

undersweeps F Major in a dance
of current joy and memory's
romance cast into mind

above my writing hand by
vast digital information empires
caught in this small device, turning

the world into my ducal music
room as the announcer tells me,
"You've been listening to *antica musica*

ensemble, La Serenissima" and I explore
the web discovering their home page
on which a painted winge'd, haloed lion

smiles welcome at all visitors above
an album called *Venice by Night*.

Sentenced to Venice

GOOGLE EARTH AND THE SERENE REPUBLIC

While walking the white dog
in what would be early-morning quiet
but for the local river's tumbling rage,

I glance toward terraced gardens of the rich –
copper canisters of purple, white and yellow
bloom beside well-crafted trees and
polished wooden furniture –

                    and wonder
                        why
I find within this live and lovely view
far less relief of that specific sorrow
                        (the one, I think,
                              you know)

than in the pigeon's view that pops up
                            in my lap

when I desire the red-tile roofs and whitish marble walls
that rim the murky waters of the Grand Canal.

Kake Huck

PINECONES, VENICE

"but there was nothing to write about/ except life and death/ and the warning sound of the train whistle." -- Billy Collins

Searching for concrete imagery,
I look out my window onto pinecones,
instead of marble, where asphalt

not water winds off to those stores and
restaurants I would enjoy much more
if only I were as rich as that poet laureate

full of wit and wine who writes of
cigarettes and sorrow but performs
like he's on Broadway while I'm stuck

staring at my front yard where pinecones with
their seeds and stickers, cement
like similes to my page and pen,

making a simple linkage I assume
you'll find profound after the punchline,
(I mean the close) when the mysteries

of home and travel (or do I mean life and death?
[and by life and death do I mean poetry?])
and our ambivalence to all that is

Italian

seems captured by the piney pitch
and Fibonacci spirals of the pinecones.

LIKE YOU, VENICE

I once ruled my corner of the earth
showing ambassadors of larger powers
that I could build and furnish fighting ships
in less time than they took to write a letter home
and now I seek no greater later years than yours:

filled with tourists weak with admiration
at my ancient spirit, picturesque in ruin,
but still working, still living, still enjoying
every morsel even as I slip into the sea.

Kake Huck

BUT NOT YET, OH VENICE

I will not see you again
until the Great Grief comes

and splits me in as many pieces
as count these conjoinéd years,

      pieces

that may only meld again
after I walk
      and walk,
            and walk
your ancient paths --

bumble down dead alleys,
stumble over marble bridges,
blunder onto water busses

going out,
      out to your islands,
coming in,
      in to your cathedrals --

losing myself as I will be lost
until the hard stone of that future's
now softens into
            then.

SENTENCED TO VENICE, YET,

For my sins of omission --
not bandaging wounds my wit scratched open,
not caring if students chose failure or success,
not having faith in the hope of justice,
not questioning romance until eruption,
not giving all my goods to the poor,
not taking up my crossness to follow

        anyone --

and so for all these sins of separation,
especially for my sins of discombobulation

grant my penance be walking these four
hundred and nine bridges, telling my beads,
hearing knees and spine clicking
complaints as I climb over water each day

toward heaven.

About the Author

Kake Huck is a desultory poet whose most recent publications include work in *Gyroscope Review* and the anthology, *Last Call: The Anthology of Beer, Wine & Spirits Poetry*. Her past work is included in the anthologies *Beyond Forgetting* and *Regrets Only* and various small literary magazines. Huck self-published a novel-in-poems about mid-Century, bisexual, wife-killer Wayne Lonergan, titled *Murderous Glamour*. Her current role as carer doesn't give Huck time for Italian travel, so she makes do with occasional visits to the canal inside the Las Vegas casino the Venetian.

www.ingramcontent.com/pod-product-compliance
Lightning Source LLC
Chambersburg PA
CBHW030132100526
44591CB00009B/623